Greed Versus Love

Greed Versus Love

An Inconvenient Truth About the Privatization of Correctional Health Care

Raquel Sanchez-Castro, MD

Library of Congress Control Number:		2010907836
ISBN:	Hardcover	978-1-4535-1237-1
	Softcover	978-1-4535-1236-4
	Ebook	978-1-4535-1238-8

This book was printed in the United States of America.

To order additional copies of this book, contact:
Xlibris Corporation
1-888-795-4274
www.Xlibris.com
Orders@Xlibris.com
81838

Contents

Introduction.. 7

Chapter 1   Genesis: Knowing the System............... 11

Chapter 2   Teaching, Healing and Uplifting 19

Chapter 3   Exodus: The Conspiracy 25

Chapter 4   Home, Sweet Home............................ 31

Chapter 5   "The Calvary" 37

Chapter 6   "The Crucifixion" 51

Chapter 7   "The Prodigal Son" 63

Chapter 8   "The Resurrection"............................. 65

Introduction

I was born during the Age of Aquarius (1971) in Puerto Rico, in what can be referred to as an ordinary, middle-class Catholic family. Ever since I can remember, I have had the strong desire to know exactly who I am and why I am here on earth. At the age of six, my mother discovered I had the gift of healing. She told me that when people who were ill came to our home to visit, I would go straight to them and place my right hand on a particular part of their bodies. Within a short time, they would be healed of their ailment.

I remember a few of these early incidents with clarity. One day, a woman came to our house. Without coaching, I went to her and placed my hand on her abdomen. A few minutes later, she started belching and muttering, "Sorry, sorry, sorry." Then, within seconds, she said, "It's gone! Thank you, my child. God bless you!" She kissed me, and I returned to my play.

Another day, my grandfather had an excruciating headache that wouldn't go away. I placed my hand on his forehead for a few seconds and then went to play. That night, my grandmother called to tell my mother that when Grandpa was taking a shower, he started to bleed through his nose (dark blood with clots). A few minutes later, the bleeding stopped and the pain was gone. He never had another headache after that incident.

When I was seven years old, my first passion became gymnastics. I wanted to do nothing else. My goal was to participate in the Olympic games and eventually open a gymnastics center. With endless practice, even while at the beach, at school or in my backyard, I became quite good at the sport. By the time I was fourteen, I was ready to try out for the national team of my country.

That's when I had the accident than ended my gymnastics' career.

I remember every detail of that goal-crushing day. I was practicing on the uneven parallel bars for an upcoming competition. I saw my mother and sister arrive to pick me up, and wanted my sister to see my routine. "Look at my exit," I shouted. Unfortunately, my body was tired and I was distracted. I flew into the air one second too late. Instead of landing on my feet, I landed on my back. Although the L5 fracture was diagnosed as being "minor," the rigors of gymnastics would be too strenuous. I could lead a normal life, but one that didn't include the activities associated with my Olympics dreams.

I went through a period of depression, feeling all my hopes and dreams had died. Nothing else interested me. Then I entered high school . . . a whole new experience replete with challenges and good times. My friends and I went out for pizza after school on Fridays, to the beach as often as possible, and even on campouts to nearby islands. After graduating from high school, I had no clear idea of what I wanted to study in college. The first year consisted of basic course, but by the second year, I was expected to pick a career. Since I was working at a casino to earn tuition money, I thought something in tourism would be a wise choice. By the end of the second year, I had developed no passion for tourism. After a session in the counselor's office for a few aptitude tests, I was told "the results show that your concentration should be natural sciences."

Surely this was a mistake. I had never been a dedicated student and my embarrassingly low grades were proof. I thought natural science courses were for "geeks" or "lab rats." The counselor stated emphatically that the academic skills part of the test showed a high ranking in scientific reasoning, and the vocational questionnaire showed I was most suited for a service vocation (aka helping others). He suggested I think seriously about a vocation in medicine. When I expressed my shock, he said that once I started taking the right courses, my grades would drastically increase.

I took his advice and my grades spiraled upward. After I graduated from college, I entered medical school in the Dominican Republic and graduated four years later with an M.D. degree. I was now a certified physician.

But all the while I studied, and although I developed a decided passion for medical service, I was still plagued by the same questions I'd always had: Who am I and why am I here? What is my life's mission?

Chapter 1

Genesis: Knowing the System

My very first job, after I finished medical school in 2000 and then a year of internship, was working as a primary care physician in an HMO center that provided services exclusively for HIV patients and doing research with new HIV medications. I enjoyed my work and the satisfaction it brought me, knowing I was making a difference in the lives of those who depended upon my training.

Soon, I took a position in the emergency room of another hospital. For five years, I worked long hours under continuous pressure. In the process, learned how to think and act quickly, calling to mind everything I had learned in medical school and my previous hands-on experiences. Again, thoroughly enjoyed the good feelings that came with the saving of lives. I wasn't averse to personally taking the time required to cut the nails of a patient with recurrent scabies in order to kill the mites hiding under the nails, or to remove a fecal impaction with my own hands when a patient was so acutely impacted that no laxative or enema could provide release. I had the ability to smell the wounds, ulcers and abscesses of patients to determine if there were an infection before the culture results came back from the lab.

One day, my uncle told me that one of his co-workers had mentioned a "great doctor" who had taken care of him at in the ER of a certain hospital. "What did this doctor look like" my uncle asked. "Is she short and blond with a loud laugh?"

The coworker had nodded. "Yes, that's the one. Do you know her?"

My uncle beamed. "I sure do. She's my niece! Next time you or one of your friends go there, you tell her you are my friend and you'll get VIP treatment."

"There's no need for us to do that," the man replied. "She treated everybody as good as if they were her own family."

My uncle said he felt very proud to be related to me.

One day, mostly out of curiosity, I enrolled in a one-year course in Chinese medicine and acupuncture. The very first day, I realized this was the "missing link" that explained all the "unsolved mysteries" of medicine for me. Traditional medical literature often defined such mysteries as "idiopathic" (an unknown mechanism of origin) or "incurable." But Chinese philosophy seemed to explain it precisely and perfectly with what it calls the five-element theory. Every pathology has its origin as an energy unbalance; its cure comes with the correction of that unbalance through manipulation of the energy flow through the acupuncture points. Soon, I was combining both therapies in my medical practice and obtaining excellent results.

I had another problem. It seemed that no matter how many days or hours I worked (usually, 24/7) during those six years, I had not been able to save any money. I was merely surviving. I still had a big student loan to pay off, my family was too poor to contribute to paying off my debt, and the conditions in my country were not conducive to solving my dilemma. The salary of a physician in Puerto Rico was equivalent to that of a nurse's salary in the USA. After much thought, I decided to emigrate to the United States. Again, since my family had no money, my grandpa made me a personal loan to help me settle in the United States (God bless him). I rented a room for $100 a week in the southeast part of Florida.

That's where I met my roommate and mentor, Dyana Hagen, who introduced me to metaphysics. I read dozens of her books about angels, universal spiritual laws, and energy medicine. Finally, I was finding answers to my existentialist questions and my life started to make more sense.

One month later, I met my husband and moved out of Dyana's dwelling to a house trailer located about 45 miles north. She gave me a big hug and encouragement to continue my journey. I applied for my physician license and, while I waited for a response from the licensing agent, collected food stamps to supplant my meager savings. My first interview was at a state prison located 500 miles northwest from where I lived; the position would involve taking care of outpatient inmates. We traveled in the middle of a tornado, at 32 degrees Fahrenheit, in a broken-down truck with no heater and a 140-pound pit bull perched on the back seat. I was asked several clinical questions by the interviewer. I answered them to the best of my ability. Fortunately, my answers met the expected standards and I was hired.

That's where my story begins.

Working in a state prison was not quite like working in the ER of a hospital. There was much to learn about state prison policies and procedures. My boss was kind, patient, and considerate. He also had the rare maturity and humility to ask me clinical questions, if he wasn't sure about a medical procedure himself. He didn't find this personally degrading. One day, he asked, "Since you've had ER experience, what's the best treatment for a toe fracture?"

"You just immobilize the toe by taping it to the adjacent toe for about four weeks." He said: "I thought so, but I wasn't sure. It's been a while since I've treated one."

In this way, we supported each other.

The nurses in the prison facility were hardworking and their acceptance of me and willingness to share hints to make my adjustment to life and work in the United States go more smoothly was greatly appreciated. I missed my family members, and they became like a second family to me.

Under the stress of our work, a sense of humor was appreciated, too. The HSA (Health Service Administrator) had an especially witty humorousness. I had never known about the existence of possums until I moved to Florida. I was afraid of them. One day, around 4:00 p.m., when we were all preparing to leave work, I heard her tapping the desktop with her fingers in a drum-like rhythm. Hearing only the sound, I inadvertently screamed aloud.

She came running. "What's wrong? What happened, doctor?"

"Oh, my God," I said, shaking. "For a second, I could swear that noise was coming from a giant possum!"

She laughed aloud. We often joked about the giant possum after that, especially when we heard strange noises.

A sergeant who worked in the prison facility shared my ethnic origin. We became friends and often told jokes in Spanish to each other. She made an effort to ensure I didn't become too homesick by bringing me food like my mother would cook. In return, I helped her heal her carpal tunnel problem through acupuncture.

Working in corrections is a whole different world for everyone involved, but especially for medical personnel. Either they love it or hate it. Within only a few weeks, I knew I was going to enjoy the experience. I found it both interesting and educational, to say the least. Some inmates gambled with food and cigarettes. Some assigned certain inmates with a different sexual orientation to be their mates. Some were very respectful, polite and obedient, others quite rebellious and difficult. Some liked to work out, others were talented artistically and designed tattoos, others manufactured tattoo machines out of tape recorder parts or any other electric device available, like a razor.

Once, I saw a patient with a penis infection, because he had cut it and inserted a pearl under the skin. I asked him the purpose and he said it was to stimulate the "G-point" of the vagina, thus increasing sexual pleasure. I'd never heard of such a thing before. Another day, I saw an inmate who wanted a sleeping pill. "Are you having trouble sleeping?" I asked.

"I've got a roommate who yaks the entire night on a cell phone with his girlfriend."

"How is it that this roommate can keep a cell phone without being caught during the random and frequent security searches?" I asked. To my knowledge, cell phones were against the rules.

"Well, doc, this is the way it goes. We pay money to the homosexuals to hide the cell phones in their rectums."

Naïve about such things, I was properly shocked, but I learned he was speaking the truth. It wasn't long after that when an inmate was sent to the hospital after being stabbed in the abdomen. While taking the necessary X-rays, the technicians saw a cell phone in the patient's rectum.

Many inmates have severe anger management issues and are overly sensitive to criticism, controversy, or what is perceived as discrimination. The result is defensiveness and, often, volatile behavior. Out of self-defense, I learned to treat them with respect and kindness and, in turn, they gave me theirs. My family had taught me to treat others as I would want them to treat me. It is a biblical principal, sometimes called the Golden Rule, and one that has always worked for me.

Other inmates have severe mental health problems and engage in odd behavior, like self-mutilation. This is a problem in which individuals feel overly anxious and their compulsiveness drives them into cutting themselves. The procedure relaxes them and brings a degree of peacefulness. If they try to fight the urge, the compulsion grows and requires a deeper cut to bring about the same peace of mind. I remember one inmate in particular who was trying to fight the compulsion. He eventually gave in, but was immediately frightened by the volume of blood squirting from his arm and screamed for help. He almost died. His intention was not to kill himself, merely to derive the mental peace that came with the dangerous practice.

Those who really want to kill themselves don't call for help. One of the prison officers found an inmate lying in a pool of blood, unconscious. When he was brought to the clinic, I found him pale as milk, with a faint pulse and low blood pressure. The lethal wound was to the right brachial artery, the major vessel that runs from the shoulder to the elbow. Fortunately, he survived after receiving several stitches and IV fluids. Although he had lost a lot of blood, he didn't need a transfusion.

When the patient recovered, I asked him why he had attempted to kill himself.

"Doctor," he said, "I've got myself a life sentence. It don't matter if I'm not the same person I was when I made all those mistakes that put me here. I've had a lot of time to think about my wrongs and I wanna make up for 'em by doing a lot for my family, my community and my world, but I won't be able to cuz I'm here. I don't have a second chance. So when nobody's looking, I'm gonna try again. Only this time, I'm gonna make damn sure I don't wake up."

Chapter 2

Teaching, Healing and Uplifting

One of the methods I use when working with my patients is to explain what is happening in their body in response to the infection or disease or broken bone or whatever the problem may be. Some doctors feel a patient with little education or understanding of how the body functions can't understand the details. I don't believe this. I use simple analogies or what I call the Sesame Street Way. I can usually tell if my patients understand by their feedback. "I got you, doc." Or sometimes, "I feel you, doc."

One of my young, healthy prison patients was absent a history of any disease. He had a slight increase in BUN, creatinine (a chemical waste molecule that is generated from muscle metabolism), sodium and chlorine. His urinalysis showed an elevated specific gravity and his specimen was dark yellow. His physical exam was unremarkable, except that his skin was dry. I asked him if was drinking enough water.

"Before I got here, sure; since I got here, no. The thing is that I was told the water in here is like poison."

"I admit that the water here isn't the best of the world," I said, "but it won't kill you if you drink it. On the other hand, if you don't drink it, you can die."

His eyes widened. "Why's that?"

"I'll give you an example," I said. "What's your occupation?"

"I'm a mechanic."

"What happens to a car if you never put oil in it?"

"Well, eventually the engine runs dry and conks out."

"Your body's engine is made up of many parts, like your kidneys, your heart, your liver, and other organs," I said. "The oil you need to keep them functioning correctly is water. Our bodies are about 62 percent water by weight. We can go without food for a long time, but not without water. When we become dehydrated, our organs eventually stop functioning."

"I'll start drinking more water then."

Two weeks later, his labs were perfect and his skin was moist.

One day I saw a patient with dangerously high blood pressure. I reviewed his chart, and noticed that he tried various anti-hypertensives, except for vasodilators. I told him that I was going to change the medication.

"You can do that, doc, but I'm not gonna take it. All those medications I've tried don't work. What makes you think a different one will?"

"Everybody is different," I said. "Blood pressure can increase for various reasons. I think your case is a matter of vasoconstriction. That's a big medical term, so I'll explain it in a way you can understand. What's your occupation?"

"I don't work."

"Then what's your favorite hobby or chore?"

"Washing my car."

"Okay . . . so what happens when you cover half of the end of the hose with your thumb?"

"Well, it makes the water pour out harder."

"And what happens when you release your thumb?"

"The pressure goes down."

"A vasodilator medication works the same way as your thumb; it decreases your blood pressure."

He nodded, "Okay, I get it now. Makes sense. I'll try it."

Two weeks later, his blood pressure was normal.

As a physician, I try to uplift my patients with messages of inspiration, along with my medical treatment. When working with a patient who had cut his brachial artery in a suicide attempt, I told him, "Hey, the first thing you need to do is stop thinking and talking like that. They can take everything from you except your thoughts." I shared the knowledge I had learned from a book by Esther and Jerry Hicks, *The Teachings of Abraham and the Law of Attraction.* "You're the sole owner of your thoughts and nobody can touch that," I told my patient. "You will attract to your experience whatever you make the focus of your attention. So, start visualizing yourself doing the things you like with the people you like, at the places you like, and by the law of attraction, you'll attract that to your life experience. In the beginning, this process may be difficult, since you're used to your old habit of focusing only on your current reality, but when you catch yourself thinking negatively and feeling bad about it, replace those thoughts with the good thoughts. Within a week, you'll notice you're getting good at it, and you'll start to see miraculous things happening in your life. If you don't believe me, just do it, because it feels better than thinking negatively."

My patient decided to give this a try. It seemed to work for him. He never attempted suicide again during the time I worked at the prison facility.

Inspirational encouragement works with HIV patients, too. The immune system is highly related to our emotions and moods. The goal of an HIV patient is to maintain a normal immune level of CD4 over 500 (below 200, the patient is susceptible to a plethora of viruses and bacteria encountered in daily life) and to control viral replication (viral load undetectable). Once the patient starts the HIV medications, the goal is to bring the viral load to undetectable levels. Health providers struggle to improve the patient's immune system. Why is this so difficult after the viral load is undetectable?

The answer is: the Placebo Effect. What does this mean? In any legitimate scientific experiment using drugs, the study must be conducted with two groups of patients: one receives the medical drug and the other group receives a placebo (a fake pill containing no medication). In some experiments, Neither the patients nor the doctors know which patients are receiving which "pill" . . . the real one or the placebo. Scientists have learned after years of such controlled studies that a certain number of patients improve taking only the placebo. Why is this possible? Because our minds can fool our bodies. It comes from the power of suggestion. Often, if we believe we are receiving the medication that will lessen our pain or improve our physical condition, we produce the same results as those who take the real medication. That's right. Even we doctors are amazed at such results. That's why I always try to combine my power of thought with the HIV patient's power of thought, along with the proscribed medical treatment. "I want to give you some homework," I tell my patients. "For the next three months, I'd like you to think positively. Tell yourself every day that you are healthy and happy. Tell yourself often and believe it!" I explain the power their thought processes have on their recovery and the Law of Attraction. Some of them become more hopeful, some of them are doubtful, but all of them understand it. No exceptions. After three months, they come in for a follow-up appointment and most show a significant improvement in their immune system (an increase in CD4).

Even those who held a strong skepticism improved. They were surprised to see the proof in their next laboratory results. Those who went about the exercise with a deliberate determination and a strong expectancy of positive results (aka faith) showed a more significant improvement. They weren't at all surprised by the lab results; they were excited. "I knew it. Yes!" they'd say, pumping their fists into the air.

Of course, this process can work the other way, too. For example, a patient whose HIV had been controlled for a long time, with an undetectable viral load and a long consistency of CD4 over 500, suddenly experienced a drastic drop in his CD4 (viral load still undetectable). I asked him if he was taking his medications or if something new had happened in his life.

"Unfortunately, doctor, my wife left me to marry somebody else."

Our immune system is directly influenced by our emotions and moods. We talked about his feelings and the importance of removing negativity from this thought processes. A couple weeks later, his stats had returned to their former balance.

Chapter 3

Exodus: The Conspiracy

Unexpectedly, I received an offer from a semi-private state prison (which means that all the budget support comes from the state, except for the salaries of the health care personnel), to take care of outpatient inmates. The facility was located about 500 miles southeast of where I currently lived. I was told the work would essentially be the same as I was doing, but they were offering 65-percnet more in salary than the state. I believed them and decided to accept the offer. On my last day of work, my friends threw me a farewell/baby shower party, with gifts, cards and cake. I cried. It would be very difficult to leave a place where I had received such warm acceptance and support. But I felt the extra income would come in handy, with a baby on the way.

Thus, my husband and I packed up and moved once again.

As soon as I began working, I noticed that few in the facility were following the guidelines; in fact, most of the staff didn't knew what the guidelines were. It was my opinion that the HSA didn't know what he was doing. He said he was a medical doctor from Mexico. I often doubted his credentials. The clerks seemed to know more about medicine than he did on many occasions. He distributed *his* tasks among the clerk staff, adding to their already full schedules. They worked hard, multitasking and performing the work of more than one employee. They worked so many different tasks, no one in the company could do their job if they had to be absent from work due to an illness or a vacation. Unfortunately, the company didn't appreciate this.

One of the clerks was promoted with a supposed increase in her salary. She never received the extra pay. Another one was so overworked, she developed carpal tunnel pain in both hands. When she filed a legitimate worker's comp claim, the company staff made her life miserable; they didn't want to pay her medical bills or purchase the key board that would relieve her pain and improve her condition. Another clerk spent over ten years working in the facility and then retired; she had been unable to accumulate an adequate retirement pension, because the state had changed management companies every couple years. Another left on maternity leave. When she developed complications and had to exceed her maximum days of leave, she was fired.

There were two wardens in this facility. The first one did as little as possible, but he had the gift of speech. During staff meetings, we would address certain issues and say, "We'll take care of that." At the end of these meetings, he'd say. "Keep up the good work, fellas." That was it. Nothing changed. None of our requests were fulfilled.

The other warden was the exact opposite. He was a hard worker, fair-minded, and always took care of business. When I was dismissed from the facility, he said, "Honestly, you are the most caring doctor I've ever seen, but I don't know anything about medicine, so my opinion is no good." Since he was not my direct employer, what could he do?

The two assistant wardens were also caring and fair-minded individuals. One of them reminded me of a big Saint Bernard with grandfatherly traits. He used to pass me candies under the table during our meetings. His eyes watered the day he had to escort me out of the building, after being fired. The other one was remarkably kind, too. Once, I was seeing a patient with pneumonia, who sounded awful; both his lungs were highly congested and producing asthmatic wheezing, crackles, ronchii and rales. I treated him with the best medications we had to offer. I was confident he would improve quickly. Three days later, I saw him again and was surprised to learn he was no better. I asked him what was going on.

"What you gave me helped a lot, doc. I was feeling great during the day, but my window is broken and I have to keep it closed at night with a toothbrush. But there's an officer on the ward that don't allow me to do that. The cold comes in the window and makes me cough all the night."

This took place during the wintertime, and a cold front had swept through the area that week. I grabbed the phone and called the assistant warden. I explained the situation to him and he said, "Don't worry, doc, I'll take care of it."

A week later, I saw the patient again and, just as I expected, he was fine. "I feel like brand new. I don't know what you did, but the problem was solved. Thanks a lot."

The nurse practitioner in this facility became a good friend of mine; we shared the same ethnic origin. We made jokes in Spanish and laughed a lot. She was very dedicated to her work and I taught her everything I knew. She was eager to learn and helped me considerably in my own work.

My superior worked for the state and not for the company, so he was not my direct employer. He spent a great deal of time cleaning up the chaos at the other semi-private institutions contracted by the same company managing other southern facilities. Although I took on the added responsibility of orienting and training our staff, it became increasingly difficult, since I was only one and they were many. In addition, I had to see the patients and perform various medical procedures. I sent memos to alert the company that the staff needed additional training.

Once a company has been informed of the lack of staff training, it is my opinion that it isn't fair to then blame the staff for not receiving it. It was my judgment that the training was merely a tenth of the training provided by the department of corrections. I am the kind of person who searches for solutions, rather than pointing fingers, but the company felt threatened. Perhaps they were concerned that they could lose the contract if the staff they provided was found to be incompetent,. So, instead of providing more training to the nurses (and I offered to help with the process, since I had just come from a state facility and had memorized all the policies and procedures), they saw me as a threat to their continued contract.

One day, I was pulling a heavy cartful of patient charts and the handle came off. I fell and injured my elbow. I filed a worker's comp claim and was out for five days. I returned to work, and two weeks latter, I was fired. Fired without warning, without a conference, and without notice. I was escorted out of the building the same way a staff member would be escorted out for smuggling drugs into a facility or for having a sexual relationship with an inmate.

The reason for my dismissal? Failure to produce quality work. What was that? After working there for fourteen months with no prior evaluations or discussion of any perceived problems? The other staff members were shocked, as well as the state's auditors, including my boss, the medical director. They couldn't understand the decision, but what could they do? They were not my direct employer. That's what happens when you work for a private contractor company. They are not held to the same regulations and standards. I requested proof of my inadequacies and they produced none. It is my belief they withheld further discussion because they knew I was fully aware of all the guidelines, policies and procedures.

I decided my firing was for another purpose—a higher purpose of divine order—so I left. A few months later, I learned the company had lost its contract for management of all the state prisons and the state had once again taken over.

I hired an attorney and initiated a lawsuit against the company for illegal firing in retaliation for a Worker's Compensation Claim. He informed me that, often, after such a lawsuit is filed, the insurance premium of the company is raised and they rigorously fight against it. I didn't know that. Somehow, it didn't feel right for me to cause distress for others while under my own distress, so I withdrew my lawsuit. I knew very well that by the law of attraction, if I pushed against the controversy, I would likely receive more. I'm not the sort of person who likes to seek revenge.

Maybe, too, it was because my inner being knew it was not the right move and something better was in store for me, a higher purpose.

Chapter 4

Home, Sweet Home

Once again, I was back to food stamps and unemployment. Even though I was depressed, I had peace and the love and support of my family, both in the United States and Puerto Rico. I also have angels who watch over me wherever I go. A special friend who worked with me in corrections urged me to apply for a position at another state prison. I followed his advice and received an interview at a state prison about 200 miles north of my current location. The position involved inpatient care of inmates in the facility. After the interview, the medical director presented me with a questionnaire on clinical procedures. I answered each question correctly and quickly. He said it was the first time in his experience a doctor had completed the quiz so accurately and with such speed. I got the job, of course.

Once again, I moved to a new location and a new job. I looked forward to the challenge and the opportunity to use my medical training. From the first day, I felt comfortable and "at home." My superior was another kind man—calm, patient, humble, and most importantly, intellectually brilliant. He enjoyed discussing clinical cases with us and he treated our nurses with respect and consideration, as he did our patients. He approved our requests for special medications, tests and consultations, when a particular patient needed it. Although he received several offers from other institutions for a lot more money, he wouldn't accept them. How can you explain that? The answer is LOVE. He had an altruistic love for those he served. With a boss like that, I was able to do my work with clarity, serenity, and the confidence I needed to have when dealing with people's lives.

On my first day at this facility, one of the officers stopped me as I was walking down a hallway. "Excuse me, doctor," he said. "The patient in Bed 5 is creating a commotion. He asked me to call for you. He said you saved his life."

"He must be mistaking me for somebody else," I said. "I just started this job today and I haven't seen any patients yet."

"Maybe you should see him anyway. He won't shut up, and that isn't normal for him. He's always pretty quiet."

The officer was right. The patient was a man I had seen at the previous institution for a throat infection. His right tonsil had been enlarged and very inflamed, with white purulent patches. I had prescribed antibiotics and he ultimately got well. Two months later, however, he showed up again, complaining of a difficulty in swallowing, although he had no pain. This time, when I examined his right tonsil, it looked completely different. It was covered with what looked like a grayish thick membrane with tentacles invading the other side and it partially obstructed the pharynx. What I didn't like was the absence of pain.

I asked him if he had a family history of cancer and he said no. In my facility I didn't have the resources to perform the tests necessary to rule out diphtheria or cancer. It was a Friday, so I decided to send him to the hospital. Either diagnosis would be considered an emergency. I figured that as soon as a doctor saw his throat, he would call for an ENT consult, since the lesion was completely different from a normal infection and was partially obstructing the airways.

The next morning, a nurse called me. The patient was sent back the previous night after being treated with an antibiotic injection and diagnosed as having a tonsilar abscess. I couldn't believe it. I grabbed the phone book and started calling different hospitals until I found one that had an ENT on call. I talked with this ER doctor and explained the situation. He promised to have my patient seen by an ENT specialist. The following Monday, I learned that my patient had been sent back with the same treatment and the same diagnosis. I decided to do an emergency ENT consultation myself. The biopsy proved my patient had cancer. He received the required radiation and chemotherapy treatment in time to prevent the spread of the disease.

Now, this former patient greeted me with a big smile. "I've been wanting to thank you for a long time, doc, and I finally got the opportunity to do so. Thanks for saving my life."

Such a success story was not only heartwarming, it offers the confirmation and reassurance any doctor needs to propel them through the often long days. It made a great start for the beginning of my new job. My efforts to make a difference in the lives of those I served were not a waste of time.

In this new facility, everyone was on the same page—we followed the policies and procedures and found work pleasurable, because of the trust and orderliness. One day, right when I arrived at the institution, one of my shoes fell apart. I limped my way from the lobby to the first office I saw. As soon as I entered, I saw that all the desks were occupied by women (thank God!). Embarrassment over my dilemma, I lifting my leg far enough for them to see the problem. "I need help," I said. "My shoe just fell apart and I'm on duty."

"Don't worry, doctor, we've also had shoe issues." They taped my shoe together with duct tape, and I was able to make it to the nurse's station. Unfortunately, with every step I took, the tape made a noticeable noise and drew eyes to me. I tried to ignore it and continue up the stairs and down the long hallway to the clinic dispensary. An orderly heard me and laughed. "What's up with the noise?"

I gave him the semblance of a smile. "Don't ask!" I continued to the nursing station and spied my solution. Big Mama was on duty. She had been working in the facility for over thirty years and had never taken a vacation. She was the most dedicated person I had ever met. I asked if she could help me with a better solution than duct tape. She took me to the maintenance office and asked an officer to help me. She had a lot of connections. Whatever any of us needed, all we had to do was ask Big Mama. The officer put some screws into my shoe's sole and I was able to begin seeing patients.

Soon after that, my shoe came apart again. Big Mama went to another nurse for assistance and they returned with a fancy pair of flip-flops with rhinestones. They were two sizes too large, but they were comfortable and I was able to work.

One of my colleagues at this facility was a doctor from Puerto Rico, too. We became good friends. Whenever I had experienced doubts about a particular diagnosis, he would help me come up with the proper one. We used to joke with each other in Spanish and laughed a lot. It made the days go faster and with more enjoyment. It was a great pressure reliever, with the stress that accompanied our job.

A particular clerk was very efficient in her work output. She was fast and rarely offered a reason to deny a request from me. When she wasn't on duty, things were a little more chaotic. I appreciated all the help she gave me and thanked her often for being so kind. She admitted it was easy for her to be this way with me because I was one of the few people who treated her with respect and love.

I got the first red flag of suspicion about county jail's potential negligence when a patient came to us from a county jail with a colostomy bag. I asked him when he had received the surgery and for what diagnosis. He said he had Chrohn's disease. He had complained for some time about several symptoms and was being treated for IBS (irritable bowel syndrome). Chrohn's disease has many of the same symptoms, including abdominal pain, bloating, nausea, indigestion and alternating episodes of diarrhea and constipation. IBS is usually controlled with Bentyl, Zantac, inmodium (for diarrhea episodes) and stool softeners (for constipation episodes) and dietary adjustments.

But, when the symptoms persist or worsen, that's usually a red flag. An intestinal biopsy is required to confirm the diagnosis. Persistent treatment for IBS, when the real problem is something else altogether, can cause severe intestinal inflammation, and sometimes even perforation and irreversible necrosis. The patient may end up needing an extensive bowel resection. After that, the patient will have more difficulty in absorbing the required nutrients to stay healthy.

I was disturbed by the way in which this inmate had been treated. I couldn't help thinking that if were to ever work in a county jail, I wouldn't let such a thing happen. Silly me. But at the time, there was nothing I could do about it. The procedure had taken place. I knew this would only be one example of the negligence in patient care I'd see in the system. I also couldn't discount that it was often due to lack of money to support better care, which entailed lack of sufficient medical staff and diagnostic equipment. It was a Catch 22 situation.

Chapter 5

"The Calvary"

It wasn't long before I received another job offer from a private county jail located about 200 miles southwest from where I lived and worked, again taking care of inpatient inmates. I experienced a flashback. I had made that mistake once before and knew better. But, this particular company had a "good reputation," and they were offering me a fifty-percent increase in salary. Since I was the only provider for my family, I was literally surviving from check to check. By now, I had three children, the youngest only a year old. My husband was a stay-at-home dad, I still had a substantial student loan to pay off, and I was financially helping my family in Puerto Rico.

Even though I experienced a reluctance over taking the position, I decided it was necessary. It was surely part of the divine order for my life.

I started my new job in October of 2009, and with the very first day I was made aware of certain difficulties. I was supposed to begin working on a Monday, but I received an e-mail informing me of an important meeting the Friday before this day. I was required to attend it.

This greatly disrupted our plans for the moving process. Since I couldn't use the weekend to move, because of the meeting date, and I lacked the money to hire a moving company, I hired a few friends and family members to do the packing and the cleaning while my husband took care of the baby. We rented a van to move our belongings.

I finished my last day of work at my former job on Thursday. When I returned home, afterward, my husband asked, "What happened to your face?" I looked in the mirror. It was covered with mascara, which had spread all over my cheeks with the endless tears shed during a farewell get-together organized by my friends and colleagues. I had also cried all the way home. Transitions are always difficult and they become more so, when we have to leave behind those we have come to love and respect.

We left our home that very evening, in the middle of the night, and drove the 200 miles so that I could attend the 7:30 a.m. meeting that morning. We spent even more time toting all our boxes into our new home, after setting up beds for our children. My clothing was still packed in boxes and when I dressed for the meeting, while dragging myself through the ritual, I had to settle for wearing my husband's underwear if I wanted to be on time.

I reached the facility on time. No one was there. Agitated, I called the medical director and found him still at home. He said that the meeting had been cancelled several days earlier and someone must have forgotten to notify me. He instructed me to go to the health service administrator's office. The administrator was apologetic. "I guess you didn't get the news that the meeting was cancelled. Sorry about that."

It took them three weeks to get my badge. They kept canceling my meeting with the colonel and then blaming him for all the screw-ups that, in the end, were the HSA's fault.

In the first meeting I attended, the HSA mentioned there were certain days of the month that he would be unapproachable. On other days, it would be all right for us to speak with him. I was immediately concerned. Sometimes, an issue needed immediate attention and couldn't wait even hour, let along a day or two.

The medical director had a great deal to say on just about any issue. He spoke like a politician and told each of us what he thought we wanted to hear. Then he would do the exact opposite. I tried not to let his disingenuousness bother me.

The MA (Medical Advisor) was the kind of doctor who reminded me of myself. She cared about the patients' health, was extremely knowledgeable and wasn't interested in playing games to cover any perceived inadequacies. She was formerly the medical director, but the stress of the position, the endless problems, and the conscientious way in which she performed her duties brought her to the point of wanting to resign. The sheriff offered her the important position of Medical Advisor. They created the position for her, in order to keep her on the staff. It entailed her overseeing the entire medical system and the quality of healthcare provided by the private contractor companies. She would decide if a contract would be renewed and dictated the problems that must be corrected in order for the renewal to go through. She changed from being the company owner's subordinate to becoming the company owner's boss. They were very afraid of her, although they should have been grateful for her input and careful analysis of their weaknesses.

I worked hard at my job. I was the only provider working in the infirmary from 8:30 to 4:30 Monday through Friday. Both the male and female infirmaries had 43 beds, for a total of 86 beds. They weren't always fully occupied, but the variety of illnesses and the severity of various patient conditions required vigilance. Not every inmate patient needed to be there. The other doctors at the outpatient clinic often referred them to the infirmary. They were required to see so many patients each day, that sometimes it was easier to transfer them to the infirmary. They didn't have the time necessary to obtain a detailed workup of the patient's complaints, make a physical exam, analyze the results of various tests, and then make a diagnosis.

The nurses often felt sorry for me, because I didn't have time to eat lunch or take a break. The day before Thanksgiving, they ordered some chicken and potato salad and called me to their room to eat with them. I was deeply grateful. Too often, I got home so late, my baby was already asleep and I could not hold or cuddle her. When a great number of my patients were very ill, I had difficulty finishing all the things that needed to be done in caring for them properly. The writing up of progress notes, for instance, was quite time-consuming. I took it seriously. Others often took shortcuts. The medical director, for instance, would create progress notes with little information and so generic, that looked all the same with the difference of the date or patient name.

From my first day at work in this new county jail facility, I observed the work habits of those around me. In the ten years of my medical career, I have never seen so many workers trying to cover over their activities. It seemed to be their primary goal, pushing the care of the patients to the back seat. When you are in a hurry, when you don't care, when you become a clock-watcher, it is easy to take shortcuts and become negligent in your duties. Extremely important data is easily overlooked.

I was curious about why so many of the doctors and nurses seemed to be working as though they were walking on eggshells. Then I noticed that the patient charts contained very little information. My first patient had been admitted for contact isolation, due to multiple skin lesions with "signs of infection." The wound assessment form was completely empty except for several "x" marks on the hands, feet and face of the human figure printed on the page. There was no name or signature of the nurse taking the initial exam, nor was there a description of the type of wound, size, color, and so forth. The questionnaire contained checks denying any symptoms of nausea, vomiting, diarrhea, or sneezing.

I decided to close the chart and see the patient myself. The skin lesions were only in the hands and feet and a few in the face. They were flat, not rounded, and of an irregular shape with lacerated erythema. They looked exactly like scratch marks that had already dried and almost healed. I asked him how the injury had happened and learned he was kicked out of a shelter and had to sleep on the street. Mosquitoes had bitten him and he had scratched to relieve the itch causing the lesions, but "it's going away." I asked him about any additional symptoms and he said vomiting, diarrhea, chills and sneezing but that was going away also, because it had been several days since he'd "shot heroine." He had detoxed cold turkey in a contact isolation room for "skin infection."

Medical literature places a lot of emphasis on the fact that you can get 95 percent of your diagnosis by taking a good history during the initial interview with the patient, without the physical exam, lab tests, or any other tool. Just a good interrogatory alone can allow the doctor to reach the right diagnosis. Too many health workers fail in this aspect of the first examination. This facility was no different. They were either too busy, with too many patients per doctor, or they didn't have enough training. Some, of course, didn't really care. After all, these were criminals.

I saw a patient in the infirmary, one day, with the history of spina bifida and multiple lumbar surgeries. He was complaining of intense, chronic back pain. He had been taking powerful painkillers for a long time, including oxycodone, hydrocodone, and Flexeril, among others. I offered him a lumbar steroid injection (kenalog/lidocaine). He said he'd been given various epidurals in the past with no improvement. I told him this was different; because is didn't go inside the spine, since the problem involved the para-vertebral nerve chains. I promised him that this time he would feel improvement; I had experienced excellent results in the past with similar patients.

He agreed to try. We gave him the injection and literally twenty-seconds later, he said, "That didn't hurt none."

"Now, touch your toes," I said.

He looked at me and frowned. "I ain't touched my toes since I was a kid!"

I smiled. "Trust me. Touch your toes."

He shook his head. "I don't mean to second guess you, doc, but I know what I can and can't do. I can't touch my toes."

I sighed. "Please, just try. If you only get halfway there, that's better than nothing."

He shrugged and slowly leaned over. He touched his toes. Grinning with amazement and embarrassment, he whistled. "That's really something! And it don't hurt as bad no more!"

"You see?" I said. "I know what I'm doing."

"But how come nobody ever told me 'bout this before?"

"That I can't answer. You can't change your past, but you *can* change your future. Now you can get relief with this treatment every three to six months. You have to do your part, of course, and do back exercises to stretch it and strengthen it."

He nodded. "Have you got some pictures of how to do it?"

I told him that I would check. I went to my office and rummaged through the brochures, but couldn't find any like they have in the Department of Corrections for lumbar exercises. I still didn't have computer access in my office (it took three weeks to get computer access), so that evening, at home, I printed some literature with pictures from my own computer. The next day, I gave it to my patient and explained the various exercises showing him how to strengthen his back muscles.

A few days later, I finished my job earlier than usual and decided to go to the clinic to help them see patients. The first one I saw had a high blood pressure reading of 180/110. Normal is in the range of 110/70 to 120/80. He had a headache. He said that he wasn't taking his medication, because every time he took it, the headache worsened. The medication he was taking caused headaches as an adverse side effect. He kept complaining and asking to have it changed, but instead, he was made to sign a refusal document for the assigned medication.

The consequence for him is that he was kicked out of an educational program. In corrections, medication refusals are interpreted as a discipline problem. And if an inmate accumulates a specified number of discipline points, he has days deducted from his "gain time." Either that or he was booted from the educational programs. I told him I was going to change his medication. He started to cry. "Thanks, doctor. You are the only person in this place that understands me and is willing to help."

Another patient was admitted to the infirmary for vaginal bleeding. The ob-gyn nurse practitioner wasn't on duty, so I saw the patient. She told me she was jailed in her fifth week of pregnancy. She had spent several days with intense cramping and that the nurses kept telling her this was "normal." Then she started to pass large blood clots with the cramping and she was told, "You see? It's just your menstrual period." Since she didn't stop hemorrhaging, she was sent to the infirmary. I performed a pelvic exam and learned her cervix was enlarged, soft ("saggy"), and dilated two centimeters. I sent her to the hospital and she returned the next day with the diagnosis of spontaneous abortion. I heard her ask for copies of her chart.

Another day, the ob-gyn nurse practitioner was vocally upset, because she had received the results of a pelvic ultrasound showing a fetal death in one of the pregnant patients. She told me she had called the medical director for approval of a hospital transfer to extract the dead fetus from the patient. His response was to give the patient a pill that produces contractions to expulse the fetus and, in the meantime, to monitor the vital signs of the patient. This is a serious procedure. What if the patient developed a uterine hemorrhage or uterine rupture, and how would she know if fetal parts remained in the uterus? Unless the uterus is entirely emptied, infections can ensue.

Another patient was diagnosed with end-stage renal disease and end-stage hepatic disease and was getting abdominal paracenthesis (the removal of fluid with a needle) once a week before he was arrested. When he arrived at the jail, he had to wait for two weeks for the procedure. He was sent to the hospital more often only if he cried. I offered to do the procedure on a weekly basis, with the patient's and the MA's approval, but the supplies never arrived during the time I worked there. They may never had been ordered. This is a simple procedure and should be administered as often as needed for any patient needing it, even if he or she is a criminal in the jail or prison system.

On another occasion, I saw an inmate admitted in contact isolation for MRSA cellulites/abscesses on the wrist, with severe edema extending to the hand and arm up to armpit. He said that it started like a pimple and start growing and getting worse, and he kept paying for various sick calls and all he was getting was Motrin. I double-checked his medical chart and saw the various sick-call requests with the handwriting of the inmate with the stories that he described to me.

Another day, I saw two patients; the first one was in contact isolation for abscesses/cellulites of the right knee. He told me the same story—that he repeatedly complained when the abscess was small and then as it grew larger before he was finally seen and treated. The second patient had been diagnosed with lupus, scleroderma and acute Reynaud's disease . . . all autoimmune diseases. He had already lost all of his fingertips, due to the poor blood circulation brought on by Reynaud's, which causes severe vasoconstriction of the hands in the presence of cold. Now, his right hand was turning black and blue with pain and decreased range of motion. I started him on prednisone, but his room was very cold.

I decided to talk with the medical director about the various things I needed to perform my job better. I told him I needed warm gloves for the inmate with Reynaud's. He told me to order the gloves and I did it; but, a few days later, a nurse told me that he denied the request for the gloves. I mentioned my concerns with the x-ray reports that were not corresponding with my clinical findings. For example, the report accompanying an x-ray of a patient's elbow said it was normal, but upon physical examination, it looked swollen and "puffy." Consequently, I sometimes had to ignore the x-ray report and go with my clinical judgment. In this instance, I extracted over 10 cc of blood from the injured elbow.

The x-rays of another patient with multiple traumas returned with a 'normal' report; even after I had received a fax from the hospital, where he was eventually admitted a few days earlier, saying he had orbital, rib and hip fractures. In another case, a chest x-ray was reported as normal, but the patient had three stents.

The medical director said that when I receive inaccurate x-ray report readings like these, I should give him the names. "I have already memorized the three names, sir. The first one is such and such, the second one is—"

"No, *next* time it happens, you tell me," he said.

I had to bite my lip. How many times does malpractice have to occur before firm action is taken to correct the problem?

I went on to discuss the two additional episodes of the patients with abscesses. He said I should refer them to the grievance coordinator. How does that help in reducing the MRSA's statistics? In the department of corrections, any suspicious skin lesions are treated free of charge, as the inmates don't like to spend their little canteen money on sick calls and infections can spread throughout the facility, even to the staff.

I also mentioned to the director there was a tendency for those in charge to focus on pointing fingers rather than solving problems. "Isn't it more effective to investigate the origin of problems and solve them, rather than firing innocent employees and leaving the problems unsolved?"

"I know what the problems are," he said. "We have a few competent staff members and a bunch of nurses who are essentially idiots and imbeciles. They screw up everything. Then the few with heads on their shoulders fix everything."

In my opinion, the majority of nurses working in the jail system are hardworking individuals who care about their patients and provide them with quality service. The problem is that they are hindered by inadequate training and the supplies necessary to fulfill their obligations. Most ask questions, when they are unsure of a procedure and are eager to please doctors.

During one of my meetings with the medical director, I mentioned the inmate who had arrived at the jail with a full set of teeth and returned from the hospital without them, and the difficulty I was having trying to get the biopsy results of a tumor they found on his lung biopsy. "Don't try so hard to be a hero," he said. "It's best not to start something if you can't finish it."

I was left to wonder exactly what that meant.

The director explained that county jails are different from state prisons. "The inmates stay for a short period of time, usually less than a year. A lot of them stay only a few days or weeks. So, while they're here, we just try to solve their problems temporarily, the cheapest and fastest way possible to buy them some time until they either go home or get transferred to prison. We're on a budget that comes from taxpayers. If we start investigating every illness for the correct diagnosis and then provide state-of-the-art treatment, costs would skyrocket. Plus, we don't have the staff or the time to devote to missionary care. If we find something serious, we have to treat it, and that becomes an expense we can't meet. It's best not to get that involved."

But health care is not a tire-repair shop, where a customer without the money gets a patch and the one with the money gets a new tire. In the treatment of human beings, regardless of their status in life, a timely diagnosis could be the difference between life and death. Even if the inmate has a short stay in the jail, we should provide the same care we would to any other person who comes for relief of his symptoms. By providing the patient with a definitive diagnosis, and discussing the benefits and the risks, any foreseen complications, and the alternative treatments, he or she can face the future with the facts and not ignorance.

Sometimes, patients would say, "I'll be out of here in seven days, doc. What should I do?"

"Well, as soon as get home, go to your doctor right away and tell him what we've discussed. Get an MRI or ask to see the gastroenterologist." Of course, most of these patients don't have a doctor and will likely end up in some hospital emergency room.

But not in our county jail systems. Patients here receive a Band-Aid. I finally understood why I had received so many inmates at the state prisons with complicated or advance medical conditions. And why the company was getting wealthier every day and the Department of Correction was getting poorer.

Very quickly, I noticed that when I spoke with the medical director about work issues and clinical cases, or sought his input on making improvements in the department, he'd clam up and try to change the subject. However, if I asked him about his travels throughout Europe or the Broadway musicals he had seen, he was more than chatty. I chose to believe that he was a good person who needed to put his job first. He had to report to those who were in charge of the budget. If he were the medical director at a state facility, the story may have been different. For the most part, he was supportive of my efforts . . . at least in those beginning weeks.

One day, a nurse mentioned that our medical director was the infirmary doctor for years and only held his current position for the past couple months. She said most nurses were wary of upsetting him, because he had a notoriously bad temper and yelled at them for insignificant things. It was hard for me to believe. I had witnessed none of this. I asked for an example. She said that when he got angry he would become verbally abusive. He would shout, "Are you f-ing kidding me? Are you an idiot!" She said they had lost one of the best medical assistants they had ever had because of him. When she had finally endured enough of his abuse, she simply walked away one day and never came back.

Another nurse had worked in the facility for sixteen years and could count thirty-eight health service administrators during that time. She had lost count of how many doctors had come and gone during that time, finding themselves fired for no good reason. I asked why someone like the director had survived in such a system for so long. The reason? He was a friend of the management company owner.

That day, I wanted to leave myself. Only the thought of providing for my family kept me there. I am the creator of my own reality. I decided to make time for a more intensive meditation and prayer.

Chapter 6

"The Crucifixion"

A patient came into the jail with only a history of sleep apnea and morbid obesity, but she was complaining of right-side chest pain, although she had no shortness of breath or diaphoresis, and her skin was not pale. The right thorax was tender under palpation, but her EKG was normal. I treated her as having costocondritis, which is an inflammation of a rib or the cartilage connecting a rib. It's a common cause of chest pain. I also ordered lab tests. The next day, I was summoned to the female infirmary, because this patient was having a heart attack. This time, she was pale, with profuse sweating, and she was experiencing left arm numbness. The EKG was completely different from the one only a day before; it showed obvious ST elevation and an acute myocardial infarction.

I started the algorithm for angina and called 911. The crash cart had no morphine. As a matter of fact, there was no such a thing as a crash cart available. In this infirmary, the 'crash cart' consisted of a carry-on suitcase filled with gauzes, bottles of nitroglycerine and dispensable needles and few ther things, but no morphine or dopamine or bicarbonate. Instead of a vial of epinephrine, only an epi-pen was available (allergic people carry one of these with them and inject a small dose subcutaneously), but this was woefully inadequate in the case of a cardiac arrest. Instead of hypertonic dextrose, the case contained only a tube of glucose paste. Immediately, I wondered what would happen if the patient were unconscious and couldn't swallow. When someone has an extremely low level of glucose, it has to be administered via an IV push in seconds, or they could die.

Anyway, I continued performing the angina algorithm while waiting for the ambulance. In the meantime, I also started a Reiki massage, which is therapeutic touch; (without touching the body about 1 to 2 inches away from the skin) it was being utilized in one of the local hospitals to improve the energy circulation in a particular area, in this case, the chest. One staff member from detention watched me. "I'm curious, doctor. Exactly what are you doing,"

I explained to him and he just said, "Interesting."

By the time the ambulance arrived, the patient already looked better, but she spent a week in the hospital, because her myoglobin was high. She was told it was 'nothing' and when she inquired as to why her EKG was abnormal, she was told that one of the electrodes had come loose from her skin. I was startled to hear this. If one electrode is off the skin, it will print a flat line on that lead, not a ST elevation.

After the ambulance left, the medical director told me not to speak with anyone from security about Reiki or energy massages, because "they are too stupid and wouldn't understand. Don't throw pearls to the pigs."

A patient was admitted for uncontrolled diabetes and advance HIV/AIDS. Her chart contained very little information, but I noticed she was on an HIV medication that is effective only if the patient is treatment-naïve or if the disease was not very advanced. Her total CD4 had been 64 one month earlier. She had what we call 'wasting syndrome' with memory loss, weight loss, oral candida (yeast infection), depression, and her diabetes was uncontrolled and fluctuating between 300 and 500.

I decided to attempt an immune reconstitution, because her HIV condition was making her other conditions worse, including her hepatitis C. I ordered CD4 labs, which were never completed. I asked if she had a tendency towards diarrhea or constipation (to decide which HIV medication to give her) and she said she was experiencing chronic constipation. I switched her to a more powerful rescue medication that has a tendency to produce diarrhea, but always provided quick and good results in immunologic reconstitution; in addition, the side effects could be managed.

One day, the MA (medical advisor) came to the male infirmary to see another patient and asked me about the HIV patient. We discussed her case; I told her about the diabetes. She said she was unaware of the diabetes, that the woman had not been shown to have it on previous visits. She said that, in the past, she had been given HIV-induced thrombocytopenia requiring various platelet transfusions. Since no mention had been made of this in the progress notes, I was unaware of this problem. We agreed to keep each other posted about that patient.

Several days later, the patient developed a urinary tract infection and was vomiting and had become very weak A patient in the advanced stages of AIDS is susceptible to infections of all sorts. When I saw her, she was not her usual self; she was lethargic and could barely move or talk. She was incoherent and her room smelled like vomit. The only thing she could say with clarity was that this had happened before and she was sent to the hospital for a platelet transfusion. I ordered fluids and labs stat, but no one could get an IV access on her because of her dehydration.

The assistant health service administrator was not available (he had the ability to produce an IV access on a mummy!), so I decided not to waste more time and called the ambulance. Immediately after that, a nurse approached me. "Here are her labs from yesterday, doctor." Since they looked fine, I cancelled the ambulance. But the lab results didn't make sense to me. The woman's clinical features were decidedly critical. I checked the date and discovered the lab results were *three weeks old!* Time was ticking and seconds could make the difference between life and death for the patient.

I called the MA for three reasons. First, the SOP (Sheriff's Operational Procedures) state that she had the authority to oversee the medical treatment of patients. Second, we knew the patient well, and we had both discussed her case only a few days earlier. Third, she was the doctor with the best clinical judgment. She said she would take a fifteen-minute break and come to help me. After several attempts, she finally achieved an IV access on the patient's neck and we were able to start hydrating her and draw blood for some lab tests. The patient got better and her lab results returned with a sodium count of 118.

Sodium is the only vehicle that transports glucose to the brain, and levels below 115 cause seizures, coma and death. But the management company doesn't care about that; they want approval for every hospital transport, even if it delays the saving of a life. Suddenly, the HSA showed up and was visibly upset to see the MA working on the patient. Then the director of nursing showed up, asking a dozen questions regarding my calling for an ambulance. During the six weeks I worked in the infirmary, it was the only time I had seen her there.

The important thing to me was that the patient improved. Later, I saw the results of the CD4, and just as I expected, her HIV condition had been hitting bottom. The total CD4 was 5. Her diabetes was out of control, running consistently between 300, 400, and 500. She was losing weight and her protein and albumin levels were very low. I wrote a request for glucerna, and the medical director disallowed it. In the denial of treatment letter, he wrote: "Give her biscuits." I thought it was a joke and called him. He said, "Well . . . give her Ensure then."

Again, I couldn't believe my ears, since the Ensure contained 50 grams of carbohydrates and 22 grams of sugar. Instead, I ordered albumin, which he finally approved.

This patient is similar to many of the inmate population. Most are defensive, when they feel threatened, sensitive to feelings of discrimination and rejection, and resentful of the system and authorities who like to wield their power. Most, however, react positively to kindness and being treated like normal human beings. With me, this particular patient was considerate and obedient. No doctor should hold a patient's former crimes against them; we take an oath to treat the ill. Period. No discrimination. That's why some doctors can treat prisoners of war, even though they were responsible for killing hundreds of our soldiers. That's also what makes doctors in the United States different from those in some other countries. For the most part, human life is valued.

The last time I saw this patient, she was in a single cell (confinement). She asked if I would read a letter from her mother, since her vision was so poor, due to her diabetes, and the letter was written in Spanish (few people knew Spanish in this particular jail). I was busy, but stopped to do this for her. The letter was written in beautiful handwriting. It was full of hope and encouragement, urging her to hang in there. She said she was going to send her money a little at a time, because the last time she sent her $300, half of it mysteriously disappeared.

I continued reading. "My lovely daughter, I want you to know that your chicken is an adult now and has laid 14 eggs already. I'm taking good care of her, but she misses you." We started to cry at the same time. At the end of the letter, her mother wrote, "I will try to write to you as frequently as I can, since I have to write to your brother too."

"Is your brother is in jail, too?" I asked the patient.

She nodded. I told her to visualize herself healthy and happy at home with all her family doing the things she loved and the universe would make it happen by the law of attraction. She smiled and said, "Thank you, doctor."

Another day, a patient was admitted to the infirmary from the clinic for SVT (supraventricular tachycardia). This is an abnormally fast heart beat (tachycardia) caused by the rapid firing of electrical impulses from above a particular node in the heart. It is called supraventricular, because the tachycardia originates above the ventricles of the heart. As soon as the clinic personnel administered verapamil, he was normalized. That's when they sent him to the infirmary. When I discharged him, he was feeling fine. The physical exam and vital signs had been in the normal range, and he said that this tachycardic episode was only the second one he'd had in the past two years. Formerly, it occurred after he used his albuterol pump for asthma. He had used the albuterol the day he went to the clinic.

I asked him if he had ever tried any other pump and he said he hadn't. I told him that the medication in this particular pump increased the heart rate and increased the oxygen demand to the heart. I prescribed Qvar and told him to use it daily to prevent an asthma attack from occurring. I also prescribed a prophylactic dose of verapamil for his SVT (the dosage that he was receiving before was subtherapeutic to begin with) then gave him a follow-up clinic appointment in seven days, so the doctor could send him to the cardiology unit, if he decided it was necessary.

On Monday, the 10th of December, 2009, I saw a patient who was admitted to the infirmary during the weekend, after spending a week at a private hospital for infective endocarditis secondary to IV drug abuse. He was discharged from the hospital with a picc line and a supply of antibiotics to be continued for five more weeks. I reviewed all the hospital reports and the only valve damage that he had was to the mitral valve; the other three were fine, including the septum. His ejection fraction was 56% (normal cardiac function). He was stable and his physical exam was normal for his condition (a heart murmur on the mitral valve area, of course, and presenting palpitations and fever, of course). He said that he felt better than when he had been at the hospital.

When I saw him, his temperature was normal; but soon after I left, it started to rise, because the nurses didn't give him the Tylenol and ibuprofen I had prescribed. Then one nurse went straight to the medical director to inform him that the patient looked like crap. Why she didn't come to me is for only her to know. Perhaps she wanted to feel important, or maybe she knew the director better than everyone else. Or maybe that was part of the chain reaction of synchronistic events leading to this book. Or all of the above.

Anyway, he told her to take the patient's vital signs. His temperature had risen to 104, which is part of his condition, especially when he wasn't given the prescribed medications. He was tachycardic, by compensation for the fever. The medical director sent him to the public hospital . . . without seeing the patient, without reading the hospital report or test results (echo cardiogram results with of normal ejection fraction), without reading my notes (that were quite detailed), and without calling me. When the patient reached the hospital, the doctors decided to do open heart surgery.

I spoke with the medical director the next day. "Why do you think the first hospital discharged the patient with only antibiotic orders and didn't see the need for surgery?"

"Because the patient had no money."

I tried hard to understand. The message I was getting was that if a patient arrived at that hospital with multiple gunshot wounds, he would be allowed to die, if he was without health insurance or money to pay for procedures. To me that really meant that they followed the guidelines the way it should be: the patient would be given the opportunity to heal with antibiotics, before cutting his heart open, as long as the cardiac function was conserved (which it was), and the heart infection was not too extensive (which it wasn't), and the patient was strong and young (he was in his early 20s).

But, the medical director had sent him to the hospital because of an elevated temperature and heart rate. *After* they called the ambulance, they gave him the Tylenol and the ibuprofen I had prescribed. By the time the ambulance arrived, the patient's temperature was already close to normal. The paramedics questioned why they should take him when the temperature was normal. The nurse who had alerted the medical director said, "No, you are not going to do this. Take him out."

And so they did.

The next day, this nurse was very pleased with her performance. "The medical director just gave me a high-five, because the patient is going to have open heart surgery today." I thought to myself: "of course they will do surgery, it is a public/teaching hospital."

A few days later, although I thought I would never get infected with the contagious disease that the company produces—FEAR—I caught myself with all the symptoms. I was walking tentatively on eggshells, afraid of repercussions stemming from the patient's in-house treatment for the first time in my life. I caught myself double-checking guidelines and dosages, although I had them thoroughly memorized. When you are in that state of mind, you can inadvertently make errors.

Once, I was going to increase a dose of Phenobarbital in a patient with epilepsy, because of sub-therapeutic levels. The anticonvulsant dosage ranges between 90 to 120 mgs, two or three times a day. The patient was taking 30 mg three times a day, for a total of 90 mg a day. I planned to increase it to a total of 100 mg a day, divided into three dosages. I wrote the order as 100 mgs three times a day! I hadn't exceeded the maximum, because the maximum is 120 mg three times a day, and I had also ordered Phenobarbital levels every three days for 14 days, so I would be following early increases in blood levels. But still, that's not what I had meant to write—I meant 100 mg in three divided doses.

Fortunately, I have those angels working behind the scenes to help me wherever I go, and that night I received a phone call from a nurse in the facility. "Doctor, did you mean . . . ?" She repeated what I had written in the chart. I couldn't believe my ears. I'm certainly not perfect; nobody is, but I was more than upset with myself. "No, no," I said. "That is not at all what I meant at all." I corrected the dosage and thanked her profusely for taking the time to question it and call me.

Unfortunately, the next day, the same thing happened.

I was reviewing the results of several labs and noticed that one patient had very low Dilantin levels. I decided to increase the dosage of his medication. Before I wrote the order, I noticed that I had renewed it as Dilantin 300 mg, two times a day. For some reason, I felt that it was not the correct dosage. I checked the old order and it was for only once a day. I corrected the mistake and wrote it the way it should be, again thanking my protective angel for making me check twice.

In neither of these cases did I put the patient at risk, but I had made inadvertent errors. This bothered me considerably, because this had not happened before during the nine years I had been practicing medicine.

That's when I decided that perhaps I should look for another job. No one can work competently and professionally while under the excessive pressure produced in some work environments. Stress can cause untold errors. I could not accept errors that occurred solely because I was mentally concerned about the staff and the way in which the facility was being run. Not when I saw so many questionable occurrences by other staff members and when the facility chose to "cut corners" in patient care in order to keep to the budget provided by the managing company. I didn't want to join the ranks, always looking over my shoulder, always second-guessing my medical judgment, fearing the loss of my job and reputation because of some stress-induced error. I needed to stay true to myself and to my work ethics.

But, before I could act on my decision, it was made for me.

Someone had to be thrown under the bus and it was not going to be the medical director. He needed to find someone else. That is why, two days later, I received a call from the clinic doctor, who asked me several questions about "a patient" he had sent to me with SVT (supraventricular tachycardia). He sounded very friendly, but there was an undercurrent of judgment. It reminded me of the kiss Judas gave Jesus before the Roman soldiers captured him.

Approximately ten minutes after the call ended with the clinic doctor, I received another one, this time from the medical director. I was instructed to meet him in the HSA's office in five minutes. My heart leaped into my throat. My body shook with uncontrollable trembling. As soon as I entered the office, I knew my fate. The medical director sat with the HSA at the conference table with an envelope in his hand.

"We have decided to terminate your employment," he said. "It's just not working out."

I held my head high. "I'm sorry to hear that," I said. "I have worked in several correction's facilities over the past several years and I know their staff would disagree with your decision. I don't believe any medical decision I've made while here is the problem and time will likely prove me right." I accepted the termination letter and left.

Private contractor companies too often use the firing of personnel to justify perceived problems, without first making an effort to find the real difficulty. Fire someone and the problem goes away. Especially when that "someone" is the physician in the infirmary . . . the one who speaks up to point out problems, who consults with the MA, who wants to spend money in order to provide the right or better care for the patients, who can't look the other way and sleep well at night at the same time, who is too respectful to fight back in an effort to keep her job.

Chapter 7

"The Prodigal Son"

I will not say I wasn't deeply affected by this unexpected firing. I was mildly depressed, mainly because I was the family breadwinner and greatly concerned about our financial situation. Nonetheless, I was at peace with the decision and somewhat relieved that the decision had been taken out of my hand. Like anyone else in such a situation, however, I also felt the urge to do something to get my job back, but I was troubled over the working conditions that may worsen if I were reinstated. There was bound to be resentment and some distrust issues to deal with.

Remember the biblical story about the prodigal son? He had made a huge mistake and left home, and when his struggles became more than he could endure, he wanted to go home, but wasn't sure of the reception he'd receive. He was afraid he would no longer be welcome. But he swallowed his pride and went home and his father welcomed him with open arms and held a big party in his honor.

Anyway, my good friend once again supplied me with the support and courage I needed to reapply. Not only was I accepted, I was offered a substantial increase in salary. I thanked God, my friend and the angels watching over me. I was ecstatic.

The first day, I was understandably nervous. Not even medical doctors are immune from concerns over rejection. When I drove into the parking lot, my heart was pounding so hard and fast, I thought it would create a hole in my chest! My hands were damp with perspiration and shaking. When I opened the door of the staircase into the facility, the first person I saw was Big Mama. I ran to her and hugged her as though I could never let go. She had this beautiful smile on her face, one filled with welcoming love. "About time you got here," she said. "I told you that you were going to come back, didn't I?"

"Yes, Big Mama, you sure did. I missed you so much. I missed everyone and I'm thrilled to finally be home again."

My colleagues made me feel welcome, too. There were lots of hugs and smiles. "It's so good to have you back; everything will be so cool from now on." My boss hugged me, too, but didn't say anything. He keeps his emotions inside, but I can tell exactly what he's feeling by his eyes and his gestures. The clerks and the nurses expressed their pleasure at my return. I felt exactly like the prodigal son who was so overwhelmed by the warmth of the welcome he received. But that's the amazing thing about LOVE. Love is unconditional, selfless, pure and devoid of judgment. It has the power to erase all the negativity, the pain, and the injustice.

Chapter 8

"The Resurrection"

Several weeks ago, I read *Mystical Traveler*, by Sylvia Browne. It describes the various characteristics of a spiritual traveler: childhood existentialist questioning, preference for the coastlines as geographic location, healing capabilities, increased sense of humor, intense desire to help others, and often the subject of persecution. So much of what she wrote seemed to apply to me. That's when I felt the urge to write my own book. I felt I had a story to tell. Once I started the process of describing my journey to the present, I felt as though I were being channeled.

I not only felt it was the proper time for me to finally advocate for myself, but for the few angels who work in the privatized corrections facilities, including the medical advisor, the assistant administrator (who is one of the best nurses I have ever worked with and who is also a priest), and the psychiatrist (who is an uncommonly fair man, totally dedicated to helping inmates understand what got them to the prison/jail system and how they turn around their lives).

RAQUEL SANCHEZ-CASTRO, MD

I fully understand the financial constraints under which our city-, county—and state-supported facilities must work. They are given a budget. Every "spending" decision must be based upon that budget. Salaries, insurance, utilities, office expense, safety measures and so forth come first. A portion of the budget is allocated to medical and dental expenditures. The money comes from taxpayers, who include those working within the corrections' systems. I am suggesting, however, that perhaps if better decisions were made, if everyone involved worked towards eliminating the GREED, more could be devoted toward providing better health care for the inmates. I am hopeful, too, that some of the examples I write about will spur those in charge to remove the weeds from the rose garden, in order to improve the system. When everyone is on the same page and the goal is finding efficient ways to better serve the ill patients, greater satisfaction by everyone will occur and the workplace will be less chaotic, less stressful, and less inclined to involve the pointing of fingers. A staff that can work in harmony and transparency produces fewer errors. They will occur, on occasion. Again, no one on this planet is perfect and all-knowing.

Within the past three years, I have worked as a physician in four correctional institutions (two public and two private institutions). I feel I have the experience and knowledge to make a judgment as to which system works best. In Florida, the public correctional facilities run better, no matter the location.

Even though the government has a tight budget, all the referrals, consults and special tests are approved when requested by a physician, except for the rare occasions when it is initially deemed that a particular procedure is not medically necessary (NMN) or when more information is needed (NMI). In those cases, we either write a second request with more information or grab the phone and speak directly with the utilization management department. This always produces the appropriate response, no exceptions. It may take a while to receive this approval, because there are so many inmates, but the patients are always seen and taken care of during the wait. The privatized institutions approve of very few procedures, even when an inmate's life may be in danger. They prefer to severely limit specialized care. Their bottom line is—like any privately run corporation—profit (Aka GREED).

The formulary of the private contractor (PC) is not like the formulary of the department of corrections (DOC). It is almost like an over-the-counter (OTC) limited inventory. The physician in a PC needs to prepare a drug request form for most of the medications prescribed and then waits with crossed fingers to see if it gets approved. In a government facility, the formulary is considerably broader, giving the physician more opportunity to deliver better quality of care to the patients.

I have offered to perform acupuncture treatments for inmates whose illness would benefit from such a procedure for no additional cost. The needles are inexpensive (only one cent each); the treatment is fast-acting, not invasive, produces no side effects, and the results are long-lasting. Acupuncture can be used for pain management, drug detoxification and withdrawal, behavioral issues, and all sorts of chronic conditions with excellent results. It's being currently used for inmates in Europe, but it seems that the mentality in the United States is different.

Another important factor to consider is the regulating authorities. The American Correctional Association (ACA) schedules its audits far in advance. Facilities know when they will occur and are "ready" for them. If the audits were random, those conducting them would be able to identify the existent flaws, irregularities, deficiencies (and even corruption) that exist in each institution. That way they could instigate the pertinent corrective action plan (CAP) to improve the system, which is the principal goal of the audit.

Privatization of public corrections facilities is detrimental for our society. Too much power in the wrong hands leads to GREED, and the consequence can lead to corruption. Surely when individuals working in the system place personal profit above the health of human beings (even those serving time for their wrong-doings), the white-collar "crime" can have the same results as the crimes that put the inmate patients in prison! A good percentage of those in the prison or jail systems are there for "crimes" such failure to pay child support, driving while having a license suspended, or stealing something for the sake of feeding their children. When they become ill or when they enter the facility with diabetes or high blood pressure or AIDS or mental illnesses, they shouldn't be deprived of reasonable care in order for the private company to earn a higher profit.

As a physician, I have treated a wide variety of patients in both the prison and jail systems. County jails, in particular, are not filled with "bad people" who have no redeeming qualities. Many are innocent of the charges against them, but lacked the money to hire a good lawyer; many are guilty of robberies, because they were in the wrong place at the wrong time and with the wrong people. Many simply don't know better, because they grew up in the only environment they knew . . . one where they had no positive role models to emulate. And, of course, many suffer from a variety of mental diseases. Really bad people are not the majority in that particular population.

Last night, the news told the story of an inmate who was found 'not guilty' by a DNA test and was released from prison after serving thirty-five years. How heartbreaking is that? This person lost the majority of his adult life in a system that deprived him of service, of daily contact with his loved ones, and of experiencing joy. How can society ever make up for such a mistake? The only way would be if we could magically turn back time. But this man's spirit knew better and he was focusing on the here and now. He was interviewed and he said he was "happy to be back in society" and his plan was to do the things that he hasn't been able to do while incarcerated.

Prison is damaging in more ways than simply depriving inmates of their freedom. Every day, they battle things we generally loathe. They are in physical danger, because of poor hygiene conditions; the environment is filled with highly contagious microorganisms. Epidemiological statistics show that in the presence of overcrowding, the incidence of contagious diseases is very high. Since more inmates are also depressed and stressed, their physical condition eventually deteriorates. Some institutions offer gym equipment use to certain inmates and that is helping.

Psychologically, inmates suffer because they lose their privacy, their liberty to visit friends or to enjoy nature, their civil rights, and host of other mentally stressful situations. Many live in a constant state of fear, as they are made to interact with some far more dangerous inmates. Their spirits are eventually broken.

You are thinking, "They wouldn't be there, if they had obeyed the rules of society." "They had choices and they made the wrong choices."

Both statements are true. But no matter what they did or why, they are human beings, and in our society, we are understanding and forgiving. Unless we are, we can't expect to be forgiven for our own infractions.

You may also be wondering why a female physician would choose to work in corrections facilities rather than in public clinics where she can treat children, the elderly, and those from the lower economic scale. Every jail and prison in the United States has a team of local doctors, nurses, dentists and other health care personnel who serve this particular population. Most of us care less for money than service. Most of us have an above average share of compassion and the desire to make a difference while we are in this world. Most of us work with our hearts. It's called working with LOVE.

When I prepare meals for my children and they say, "Mmmm, this is good, Mommy," I say, "You know why?" They grin and say, "Because you made it with looooove." Maybe they don't fully understand it now, but repetition will be permanently saved in their minds and when they grow up they will understand the true meaning (that everything you do with love is going to be perfect)

Those who work in public corrections institutions aren't looking for special thanks or awards or daily recognition. They just want the world to be a better place. They just want to go home every day knowing they have contributed to the comfort of someone who was hurting.

I know now why I have moved so many times. It was necessary for me to experience life as a physician in different facilities, in different regions of the state (northwest, southeast, northeast and central west), and under different management schemes, working with those who didn't always share my philosophy of what constitutes good medical care. Unless I had experiences with both inpatient and outpatient groups, I wouldn't be knowledgeable of the difference in state, county, semi-private and private corrections institutions, and wouldn't know where I needed to be to fulfill my destiny. I also wouldn't have learned that life for none of us is a smoothly paved road; we all hit potholes and swerve to miss collisions and, sometimes, experience fender-benders that test our ability to cope and then carry on.

I have read that none of us know how good Paradise is, unless we've been through Hell. And we can't recognize an angel, unless you've met a few demons. I can clearly attest to the truth of this statement!

At this point in my life, I know that I have much more to learn about my adopted country, about its citizens, and its systems of medical care for those confined in corrections institutions.

I know that I am greatly disappointed in the move toward increasing the privatization of the corrections system, because it has a decidedly negative affect on the health care inmates receive (and society as a consequence)

I know that privatization focuses on profits and "greed" rather than service and "love."

It is my hope that those who read this short account of my journey—from a young Puerto Rican girl with a proclivity for healing to a practicing physician in an American penal system—will find themselves thinking about those who suffer from illnesses and diseases and are too often left with a pill, when they need surgery, or an aspirin, when they need a more powerful medication. This is the inconvenient truth about the privatization of correctional health care.

THE END

www.ingramcontent.com/pod-product-compliance
Lightning Source LLC
Chambersburg PA
CBHW020355290526
45785CB00005B/2298